Published by Creative Education
123 South Broad Street, Mankato, Minnesota 56001
Creative Education is an imprint of The Creative Company

Designed by Stephanie Blumenthal
Production Design by Melinda Belter

Photographs by Corbis, Hermine Dreyfuss, Steven Ferry, David Liebman, Galyn C. Hammond

Library of Congress Cataloging-in-Publication Data

Richardson, Adele, 1966–
Silk / by Adele Richardson
p. cm. — (Let's Investigate)
Includes glossary and index
Summary: Examines the origin, processing, and historical and modern uses of silk.
ISBN 0-88682-963-1
1. Silk—Juvenile literature. [1. Silk.] I. Title. II. Series. III. Series:
Let's Investigate (Mankato, Minn.)
TS1546.H38   1999
677'.39—dc21   98-30300

First edition

2 4 6 8 9 7 5 3 1

SILK

ADELE RICHARDSON

Creative Education

SILK
ROYALTY

For hundreds of years after silk was discovered, only members of the Chinese Emperor's family were allowed to wear it.

Right, embroidered silk fabric
Above, silk tassels

Many people have clothes made of silk. The material can be very soft and shiny—and very **expensive!** Silk was first discovered more than 4,000 years ago in China, and the secret of how to make it was kept hidden until the year 300. Today, many countries make colorful silk cloth-ing. It is so beautiful that it is often called the "Queen of Fabrics."

SILK
COLORS

Silk was once colored with dyes found in nature. Purple came from seashells, and blue from woad, a type of cabbage.

SOURCES OF SILK

Most silk is cultivated on farms. It is made by the **caterpillars** of a moth called *Bombyx mori*. The young also go by the name **silkworms.** These moths have been used in **captivity** for so long that scientists believe none live in the wild anymore. The leaves of mulberry trees are the only food they eat; a silkworm farm must have hundreds of these trees.

Some silk can be made in the wild. It is called tussah. The caterpillars of these particular moths eat only leaves from oak trees. They can be found in China and India. The silk these worms make is a brown or tan color. It's not as shiny as silk from farms. Wild silk can be very expensive because the collecting of it takes many hours of hard work. Once collected, this silk is also more difficult to prepare than farm silk.

SILK
S N A C K

About 282 pounds (127 kg) of mulberry leaves are eaten by the caterpillars required to make one pound (.5 kg) of silk.

Center, silk saris
Above, oak silk moth

SILK

One time in Sweden, skeins of silk that had been buried in mud for 27 years were recovered. After being washed and dried, they looked like new.

8

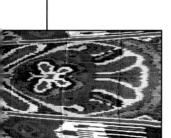

**Right, dyed silk thread from Indonesia
Above, silk cloth woven by hand**

Spiders spin their webs with silk, but it is not used for making clothes. This is because long strands are needed to make clothing, and spiders spin only short ones. Silk from a spider is much stronger than that from a caterpillar. It is used to make various items such as sewing thread, kite string, and fishing line.

The raising of silkworms on farms is called sericulture. This involves taking care of the adult moths, the eggs, and the caterpillars, and growing the mulberry trees. Farmers stay very busy making sure the silkworms are kept at a comfortable temperature at all times. They often check for any illnesses or **diseases,** and, because flies can spread harmful germs, they keep flies from bothering the young silkworms.

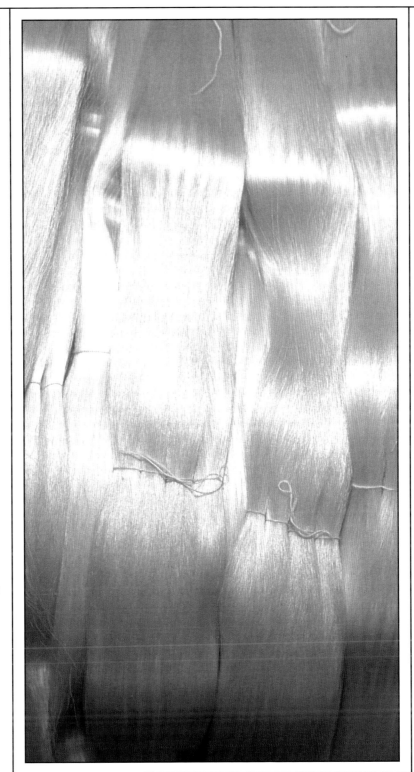

SILK
LEADERS

Even though China produces more silk than any other country, the U.S. leads the world in making products from silk.

9

Left, hanks of raw silk
Above, waterskiers
wearing silk jackets

SILK
CHOICES

Some spiders, called orb weavers, can make six different types of silk, depending on what part of the web it is needed to build.

SILK
STALKS

Chinese silk farmers sometimes use cut up wheat stalks leftover from harvest for caterpillars to spin cocoons on.

*Top, silk moths mating and laying eggs
Bottom, silkworms feeding on mulberry leaves*

The female moth will lay anywhere from 300 to 500 eggs at the beginning of summer. Each of the eggs are about the size of a pinhead. She places them on special pieces of paper set down by the farmer. A few days after she has finished laying the eggs, the moth will die.

Next, the eggs are placed in cold storage, similar to a refrigerator, until spring. When the farmer wants them to hatch, they are heated up in an **incubator.** It will take about 20 days for the tiny caterpillars to wiggle out of the eggs.

SILKWORM GROWTH

Newly hatched silkworms are called ants. They grow very quickly because they eat almost nonstop all day and night. Farmers have to bring them fresh mulberry leaves every two to three hours. This constant eating will last 25 to 30 days. During this time the silkworms will molt, or shed their skin, four to five times.

Making silk is not common in North America because mulberry trees don't grow well in the colder, dryer climate —there is nothing to feed the silkworms.

11

Mulberry leaves are collected to feed silkworms

SILK

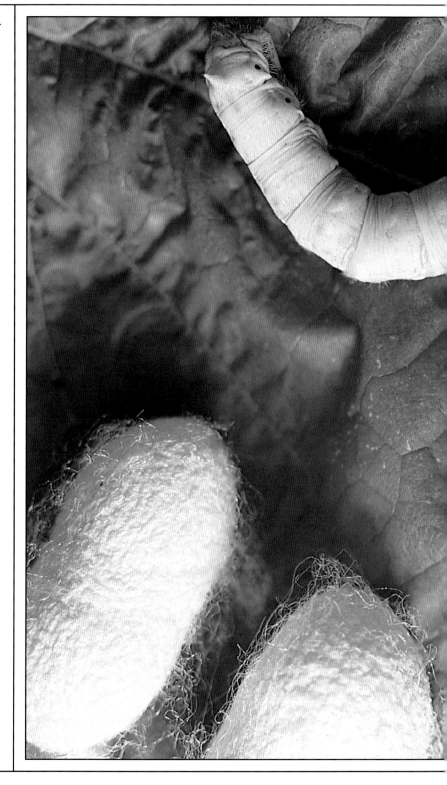

Sometimes two caterpillars make one cocoon together; it makes a thicker silk thread called douppioni.

*Above, a pair of caterpillars preparing to cocoon themselves
Center, silkworms and cocoons*

A fully grown silkworm will be about three inches (8 cm) long and one inch (2.5 cm) thick. Their bodies are a gray or yellowish-gray color. After the last molt, the silkworms stop eating. Farmers check them for any illnesses, then place them into trays that are divided up into sections. Inside the trays are tiny twigs the farmer has set there. The worm will make silk to attach itself to the twigs, then spin a **cocoon** around its body.

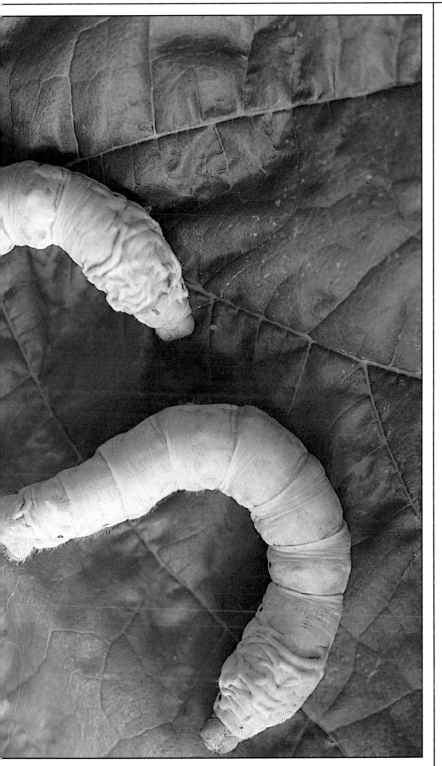

The silk comes out of two tiny holes, called spinnerets located near the mouth. The fresh silk is wet, but it hardens and dries as soon as it touches the air. Silk comes out of both spinnerets. The silkworm also makes a sticky gum called sericin that glues the two strands together, making the silk stronger.

SILK WORK

It takes about 5,500 caterpillars to spin enough cocoons to make two pounds (1 kg) of silk.

SILK BURIAL

Pieces of silk more than 3,000 years old have been found inside ancient burial tombs in China.

SILK
STORAGE

Farmers keep silk-worm eggs in cold storage to prevent them from hatching before enough mulberry leaves are grown for food.

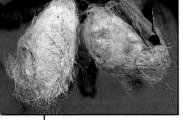

Above and right, silk-worm cocoons Opposite, silk neckties

he caterpillar makes a figure-eight pattern over and over to cover its body, never stopping until it runs out of silk. One strand can be over 13,000 feet (3,962 m) long! It takes about three days to make a completed cocoon.

SILK

T R I C K S

To keep the secret of making silk, the Chinese once told people that it came from scraping the fuzz off tree bark.

16

Center, machines reeling silk into hanks Above, opening cocoons

If the cocoons are left alone, the caterpillar will change into a moth and burst out of it in 14 to 18 days. Silk moths don't eat, and they can't fly. As soon as they are out of the cocoon, they look for a mate and begin to lay eggs. However, most of the moths are not allowed to develop. Whole strands of silk are needed to make fabric, and a moth bursting from the cocoon breaks the slender thread into pieces, ruining it.

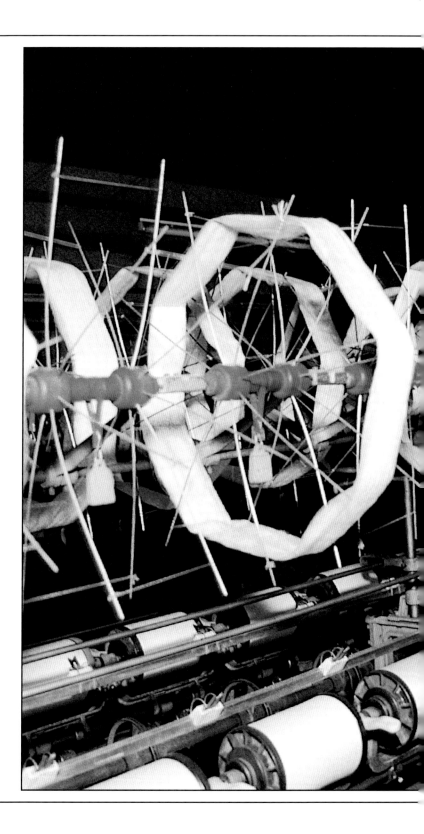

PREPARING THREAD

As soon as the caterpillars have finished making their cocoons, they are collected. The cocoons are either dropped into hot water or placed in ovens, which kills the silkworms. The silk is then unwound from the cocoons in a process called reeling.

The cocoons soak in water to loosen the gummy sericin. A gentle brushing will help locate the ends of each strand. When found, five to ten of the strands are drawn through a guide that looks much like the eye of a needle.

SILK
STRENGTH

One silk strand no thicker than a human hair is stronger than some types of steel that are made into the same thickness.

Boiled cocoons ready to be reeled

SILK
STRETCH

Silk is prized by clothing designers because when it is stretched it returns to its original shape.

Center, raw silk hank Above, silk stockings for sale in China

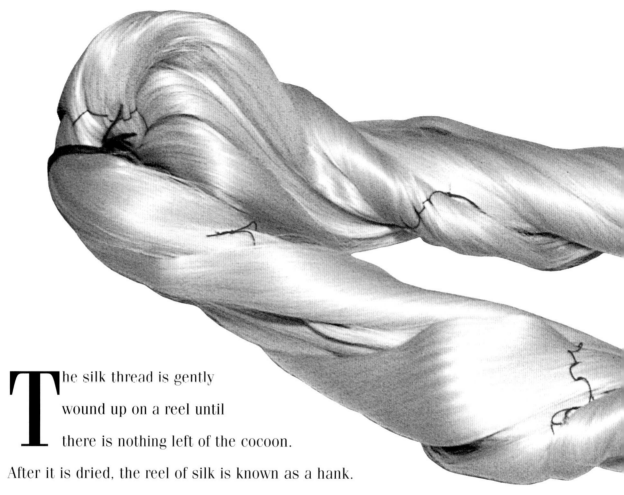

The silk thread is gently wound up on a reel until there is nothing left of the cocoon. After it is dried, the reel of silk is known as a hank.

The silk thread is stronger now than when it first left the cocoon because five to ten strands where brought together during reeling. However, it is still not strong enough to make fabric. To strengthen it, a process called throwing is used. During throwing, several strands are twisted together by machines to make one heavier strand of thread.

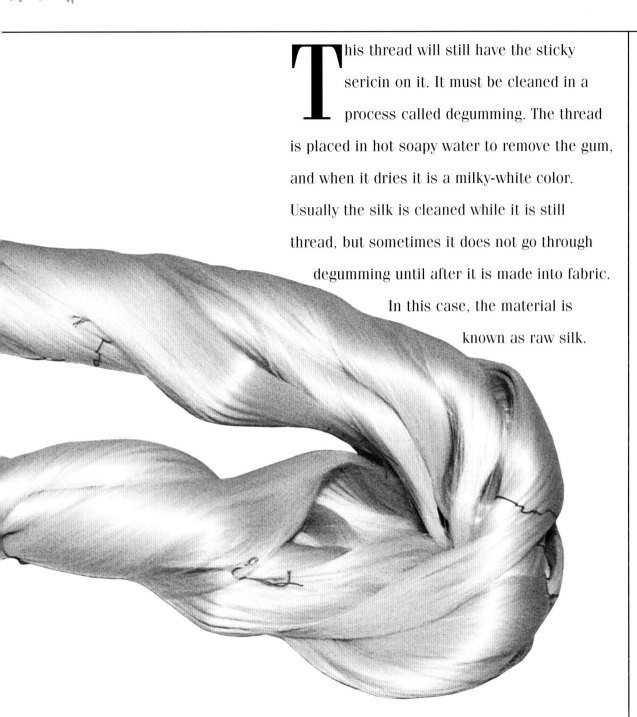

his thread will still have the sticky sericin on it. It must be cleaned in a process called degumming. The thread is placed in hot soapy water to remove the gum, and when it dries it is a milky-white color. Usually the silk is cleaned while it is still thread, but sometimes it does not go through degumming until after it is made into fabric. In this case, the material is known as raw silk.

Mutmee is a wild silk from Thailand. The strands are dyed different colors and woven by hand into pictures of things found in nature, such as trees or snakes.

Working with dyed silk

SILK
MONEY

*Silk was so valuable in **ancient** China that it was used to pay for products bought from other countries.*

SILK
WARMTH

Clothes made of silk are light in weight, but they can keep people warmer than clothes made of cotton fabric.

Silk sari

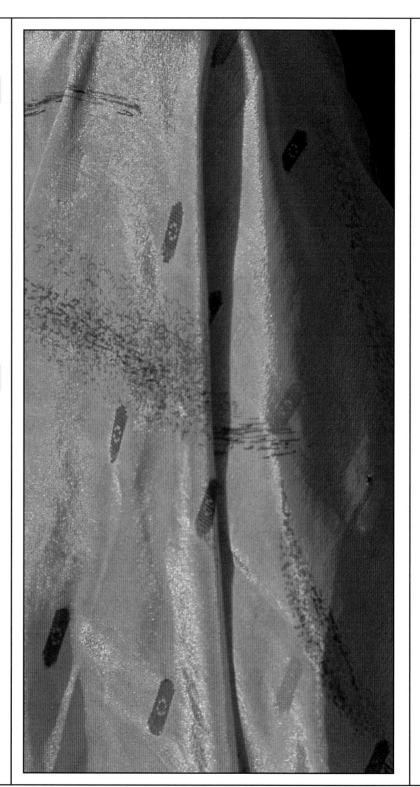

MAKING FABRIC

Silk threads must be woven together in order to make fabric for clothes. They are placed on a machine called a loom. The threads are placed in two directions. Threads called the warp are straight up and down. Weft threads are those running left and right. The machine tightly laces the threads together by moving the weft threads over and under the warp threads, making a piece of fabric.

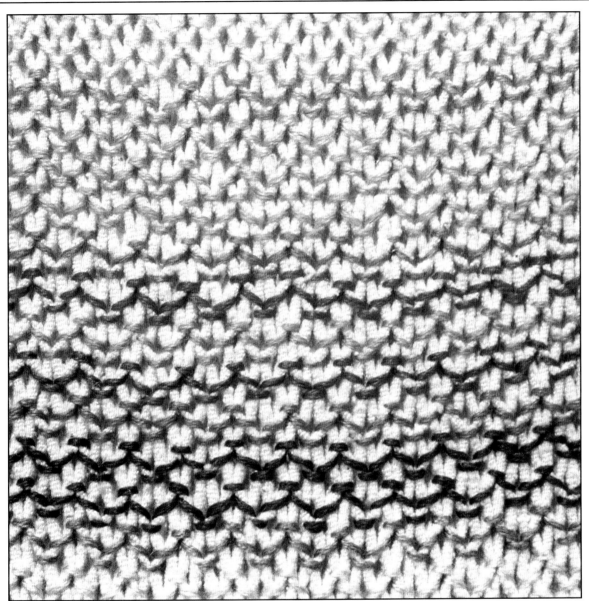

Some instruments from the Far East, such as the lute and zither, once had strings made of silk.

Many silk clothes are dyed beautiful colors. The dye is a colored liquid that the white silk **absorbs,** turning it into another color. Silk being colored before it is made into fabric is called skein dyed. If it has already been woven into fabric and ready to be made into clothes, the process is called piece dyeing.

*Left, smocking fabric made from silk
Above, lute with strings made of silk*

SILK

Right, drying silk fabric in the wind
Above, silk wall hanging

Silk is a very popular material. For many people, their favorite clothes are silky soft shirts, pants, ties, and dresses. Making silk takes time and a lot of care, so these clothes are usually very expensive.

SILK
ROLLERS

Modern reeling machines can roll up to 11 pounds (5 kg) of silk thread in about eight hours.

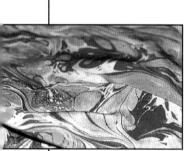

Right, handpainting silk scarves in Turkey Above, Turkish "ebru" fabric made of silk

SILK HISTORY

Silk was discovered in China sometime around 2700 B.C. The Chinese tell a story about Hsi Ling Shi, an empress who one day saw worms eating the leaves off her mulberry trees. A couple days later, the trees were covered with white cocoons. She was very curious, so she plucked one off a tree and took it into her house. As she was looking it over, the empress accidentally dropped the cocoon into her cup of hot tea.

The tea was so hot she couldn't reach her hand inside to grab the cocoon. Instead, she poked at it lightly with her finger. As the cocoon sat in the tea, it began to unwind. Once her tea cooled, the empress reached her finger into the cup and pulled out a tiny strand of silk.

Silk rug

SILK
SAFETY

Silk is a safe, heat-resistant material for clothing. It will burn only if held directly over fire.

SILK

BUILDING

The first factory to make silk clothes in the United States was built in 1810 in Mansfield, Connecticut.

SILK

SOCIETY

Julius Caesar, a powerful soldier and leader of ancient times, allowed only the people he liked best wear silk.

Bolts of silk fabric

SILK SPREADS

Hsi Ling Shi was very excited about the discovery and convinced her husband, the emperor, to plant many more mulberry trees. The empress began raising silkworms and soon discovered how to make their silk into fabric. Many believe she created the first loom. No one knows for sure if this story is true, but we do know that silk was first discovered in China, and the mystery of its making was kept a secret for many centuries!

SILK
TRAVEL

The Silk Road opened in 139 B.C. It is the name of a 4,000-mile (6,440-km) trade route stretching from China to the Mediterranean Sea.

SILK
PRISON

In England during the 1500s, only rich people could wear silk; others who were caught wearing silk were thrown into jail.

Robe of a Taoist priest from China

Many stories exist that tell how silk-making came to other countries. Sometime around the year 300, as one story goes, four young Chinese girls were kidnapped by people from Japan and forced to tell the secrets of how silk is made.

I ndia is said to have learned to make silk when a Chinese princess was given to an Indian prince to marry. As a wedding gift, she hid a mulberry leaf containing silkworm eggs in her hair. After the eggs hatched and the silkworms spun cocoons, she taught her husband how to reel the thread.

SILK
ARMOR

Long ago, Japanese Samurai warriors used silk ties to hold the metal plates in their armor together.

Jacket of a British herald from long ago

SILK
PRINTING

To decorate T-shirts, some companies use silk screens with designs on them. Ink is forced through the silk design and onto the shirts.

30

*Right, young Tibetan Lama, or holy person
Above, factory worker printing Italian silk
Opposite, customer inspecting silk fabric*

While no one can say for sure which stories are true and which have come from the imagination of story-tellers, one thing is certain: silk has always been a highly prized material with a long and mysterious history. Silk is still very valuable. It is made in several countries, and silk products are sold in stores all over the world. Today just about anyone can own a piece of clothing made of the "Queen of Fabrics."

Glossary

When something is old, was created, or existed during a time long ago, it is said to be **ancient.**

Animals kept in **captivity** can be pets or can be part of zoos or farms; they are not necessarily tame or domesticated.

The wormlike, often brightly colored, hairy or spiny wingless form of butterflies or moths are called **caterpillars.**

An area's **climate** is the average type of weather determined over several years.

Electricity is a basic energy that can provide power to run engines and turn lights on.

An **incubator** is a machine that provides heat needed for growth or development.

Caterpillars that produce silk, used in making clothes, are called **silkworms.**

When something costs a lot of money to make or to buy, it is said to be **expensive.**

Diseases cause parts of a human or animal body to fail to work properly or become damaged; some diseases cannot be treated and can lead to death.

A **cocoon** is the covering of silk that caterpillars spin around their bodies.

Any material that **absorbs** something, such as water, soaks up the water and holds it.

A **telescope** is a piece of scientific equipment that allows humans to see into great distances, across land or into the sky at night to see stars and planets.

Index